SNAKE

DICTIONARY

An A to Z of amazing snakes

Author Clint Twist
Managing Editor Ruth Hooper
Art Editor Julia Harris
Production Clive Sparling
Consultant Zoologists Robert and Valerie Davies
Illustrators Robin Carter (Wildlife Arts), Stuart Carter (Wildlife Arts), Barry Croucher (Wildlife Arts), Sandra Doyle (Wildlife Arts), Ian Jackson (Wildlife Arts), Peter Scott (Wildlife Arts), Myke Taylor (Wildlife Arts), Gill Tomblin

Created and produced in 2003 by
Andromeda Children's Books
Station House
8-13 Swiss Terrace
London
NW6 4RR
United Kingdom
www.andromeda.co.uk

Copyright © 2003 Andromeda Children's Books

Scholastic and Tangerine Press and associated logos are trademarks of Scholastic Inc.

This edition produced in 2003 for Scholastic Inc.
Published by Tangerine Press, an imprint of Scholastic Inc.
557 Broadway, New York, NY 10012

10 9 8 7 6 5 4 3 2 1

ISBN 0-439-54425-4

Printed in Hong Kong by Dai Nippon Co. Ltd.

Key to symbols
Throughout *Snake Dictionary* you will see a symbol, either a hand or a man, next to a red icon of each snake listed. The hand or man will help you to imagine the size of each snake in real life.

7 inches

The first symbol is a human adult's hand, which measures about 7 inches (18 cm) from the wrist to the tip of the longest finger. Some snakes are as small as this, so the size comparison will help you to imagine their size.

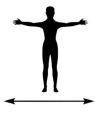
6 feet

The second symbol is an adult human. With his arms outstretched, his arm span would measure about 6 feet (1.8 m). The symbol will help you to imagine the size of some of the really big snakes.

Where you see this red warning triangle next to a snake, this means the snake is venomous and may be deadly to humans. Some of these snakes have weak venom, but all are dangerous.

SNAKE
DICTIONARY
An A to Z of amazing snakes

tangerine Press®

What Are Snakes?

Snakes are a group of reptile predators that have long bodies and no legs. They range from about 12 inches (30 cm) to more than 26 feet (8 m) in length. Most snakes live on land, although there are some sea snakes and freshwater snakes. Like other reptiles, snakes are cold-blooded and rely on the heat energy of their environment for warmth. Some snakes lay eggs, while others give birth to live young.

The reticulated python which can reach a length of 33 feet (10 m).

The Flowerpot snake which never grows to more than 6 inches (16 cm) in length.

Snake bodies

Snakes have a very smooth outline—their bodies are not divided into segments like worms or caterpillars. Some snakes have narrow heads, while others have squat, triangular heads with wide jaws. Inside their bodies, snakes have a long spine with flexible ribs, which protect the internal organs. The outside of a snake's body is covered with overlapping scales, which are usually smooth, although some snakes have very rough scales.

The stinking goddess has a slender body and smooth scales with black edges.

The water snake hunts fish and amphibians in the water.

Snake senses

Snakes do not have eyelids; their eyes are protected by transparent scales. Most snakes have limited eyesight and a few of the blind, burrowing snakes are completely eyeless. They rely on other senses to survive. Although they breathe through their nostrils, snakes get most of their sense of smell from their tongue. As it flicks in and out, a snake's tongue samples the air for any interesting molecules. These are analyzed by Jacobson's organ, which is situated inside the mouth. Some snakes have heat-sensitive pits beneath their eyes for hunting warm-blooded animals at night.

The mangrove snake seeks out frogs, lizards, and small mammals, as well as birds and their eggs.

Living and moving

Snakes live in nearly every habitat on Earth, except for the ocean depths and the polar wastes. In cool climates, snakes hibernate during the winter. In warmer climates, snakes are active year-round. Most snakes live on the ground and move by flexing their bodies from side-to-side, using their scales to get a grip on the rough ground. Some snakes live in trees, and are excellent climbers, while others prefer to burrow underground in search of prey.

The sidewinder moves quickly by flexing its body into a series of S-shaped loops.

Food Source

All snakes are meat-eaters and hunt other animals for food. There are no plant-eating snakes. Snakes cannot take bites out of their prey, but must swallow it whole. Nearly all snakes kill their prey before swallowing it, either by constriction or by using venom. Some snakes are active hunters, while others wait in ambush for their unsuspecting prey to come close enough. After feeding, a snake does not need to eat again for several days—longer if the prey was large.

Wagler's viper hunts with venom strong enough to kill an adult human.

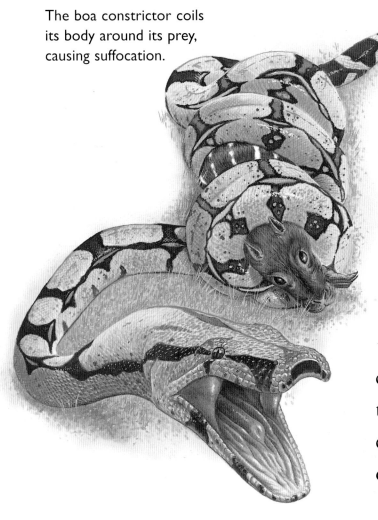

The boa constrictor coils its body around its prey, causing suffocation.

Coils of death

Some snakes kill their prey by constriction. The snake seizes the prey in its mouth and then winds a few coils of its body around its victim. The snake does not try to crush its prey, just hold it firmly. As the victim struggles, the snake tightens its hold until the victim cannot breathe. Large constricting snakes, such as the anaconda and reticulated python, are strong enough to kill an adult human, but human deaths by this type of snake are rare.

The western diamondback rattlesnake is often found on desert roads. Their venom can be fatal.

Deadly bites

Many snakes use venom to kill their prey, but not all of them are dangerous to humans. Most have weak venom that runs down fangs at the back of their mouth. They have to chew the venom into their prey. Some snakes, however, have hollow fangs at the front of their mouths that inject venom into their prey. These snakes have very strong venom, and are dangerous to humans.

Poisonous purposes

Not all snake venom is the same. Some snakes, especially those that hunt birds, need a very fast-acting venom. If it works too slowly, their prey may still escape after being bitten. Other snakes have fairly slow-acting venom and have to wait patiently for their victim to die. The antidote to a snake bite (sometimes called an anti-venom) is made from the venom itself. The venom is collected from live snakes, by a dangerous process known as "milking."

The copperhead kills frogs, lizards, and small mammals with its venomous bite.

Snake Types

The are approximately 2700 species of snakes in four main groups. **Boas and pythons** form one group, and they all kill their prey by constriction. Most snakes belong to the widespread group known as **common snakes**, most of these are nonvenomous. **Cobras, kraits, coral snakes**, and their relatives form a group called elapids. They are equipped with fixed fangs at the front of their mouths for injecting venom. **Rattlesnakes and vipers** are considered the most highly developed group of snakes, and have hinged venom fangs at the front of their mouths. All front-fanged snakes are dangerous—if you see one, stay away!

Rainbow boa

Boas and pythons

Boas and pythons tend to have thick bodies and, along with the blindsnakes, are considered the most primitive snakes. Some boas and pythons have heat-sensitive organs for locating their prey.

Common snakes

Common snakes are the most widespread and numerous snakes. They include garter snakes, racers, and king snakes. A few kill their prey with venom, but the fangs are in the back of the mouth and are not efficient. Only very few common snakes are considered dangerous.

Cat-eyed snake

Arizona coral snake

Cobras, kraits, and coral snakes

Cobras, kraits, mambas, and coral snakes vary considerably in size, shape, and color, but all have one feature in common. Each has two hollow or grooved fangs fixed in place at the front of the mouth. There are a few snakes that spit venom. The snakes in this group are known as elapids.

Malayan pit viper

Rattlesnakes and vipers

Rattlesnakes and vipers have the most dangerous teeth in the world. Their hollow front fangs fold flat when the snake's mouth is closed, which means that the fangs can grow longer—and inject venom more deeply—than those of other snakes. Some of the snakes in this group are known as pit vipers.

Aa

Adder ⚠

The adder (*Vipera berus*) is a true viper. This poisonous snake is found across Europe and Asia and as far north as the Arctic Circle. It is the only snake that can live year round in the Arctic. It is easily identified by a broad zigzag line down its back. The adder injects a fast-acting venom to kill its prey. It is not usually strong enough to kill a healthy adult, but it is dangerous to children and the elderly.

Max length: 2 feet (60 cm)
Vipers

Aesculapian snake

Max length: 6 feet (1.8 m)
Common snakes

The Aesculapian snake (*Elaphe longissima*) is found across most of southern Europe. It is nonvenomous and lives around the edges of forests and fields. The Aesculapian snake feeds mainly on small birds and mammals, which it kills by constriction.

Fact
The Aesculapian snake takes its name from Aesculapius, the ancient Greek god of medicine, whose symbol was a snake twined around a staff.

Max length: 30 feet (9 m)
Boas and pythons

Anaconda

The green anaconda (*Eunectes murinus*) is the world's largest snake and can weigh up to 550 pounds (250 kg). It lives in the rainforests of South America and spends most of its time in shallow water along riverbanks. The green anaconda feeds on mammals such as deer and large rodents, trapping its prey in its thick coils.

Max length: 3 feet (90 cm)
Common snakes

Antiguan racer

The Antiguan racer (*Alsophis antiguae*) may be the world's rarest snake. It was once widespread across the Caribbean island of Antigua, but is now found only on two very small nearby islets. The Antiguan racer prefers a forest habitat, even though it is not good at climbing trees. It feeds mainly on lizards, which it hunts on the forest floor.

Max length: 1 foot 8 inches (48 cm)
Elapids

Arizona coral snake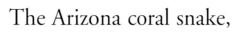

The Arizona coral snake, (*Micruroides euryxanthus*) also known as the western coral snake, is a small, venomous snake found in the southwestern United States and northern Mexico. It spends most of its time in its underground burrow.
Coral snake venom can kill a human, but it rarely strikes people.

Max length: 4 feet (1.2 m)
Vipers

Australian tiger snake

The Australian tiger snake (*Notechis scutatus*) is found in southeastern Australia, where it feeds mainly on frogs that it hunts during the day. This snake is highly poisonous and is considered very dangerous. Its venom is strong enough to kill a person, if medical treatment is not given.

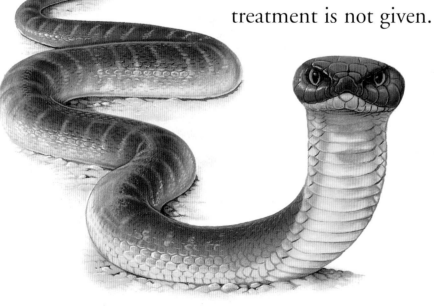

Fact
Tiger snake anti-venom must be taken quickly, if a bite is suspected, because the venom can have a fatal effect in as little as thirty minutes.

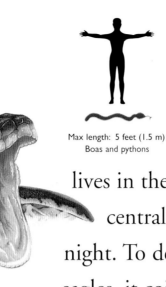

Max length: 5 feet (1.5 m)
Boas and pythons

Ball python

The ball python (*Python regius*), also known as the royal python, is a nonvenomous snake that lives in the equatorial regions of western and central Africa, where it hunts small animals at night. To defend itself from predators, such as eagles, it coils its body into a tight ball, which is why it is known as a ball python.

Bandy-bandy ⚠

The bandy-bandy (*Vermicella annulata*) is a small Australian snake related to kraits and

Max length: 2 feet (60 cm)
Elapids

mambas. It spends the day underground and emerges at night to hunt other snakes. Although it is poisonous, it is not considered dangerous because it injects very little venom.

Blindsnake

Max length: I foot 6 inches (45 cm)
Common snakes

Schlegel's blindsnake (*Typhlops schlegeli*) is one of more than 160 species of blindsnake that are found throughout Central America and northern South America, sub-Saharan Africa, southern Asia, and Australia. Like other blindsnakes, this is a small, burrowing snake that feeds on termites and other invertebrates.

Blood python

Max length: 6 feet 6 inches (2 m)
Boas and pythons

The blood python (*Python curtis*) is the name given to the brightly colored variety of the short-tailed python found in the forests of Southeast Asia. This nonvenomous snake lives among the leaf litter, where it ambushes birds and small mammals. It has a powerful bite and can be aggressive if disturbed.

Blue Malaysian coral snake ⚠

Max length: 5 feet (1.5 m)
Elapids

The blue Malaysian coral snake (*Maticora bivirgata*) is found in the tropical forests of Southeast Asia. It is extremely venomous and is sometimes called the "100 paces" snake, because that is supposedly the farthest a person can walk after being bitten. The bright orange markings are a warning that this snake is very dangerous.

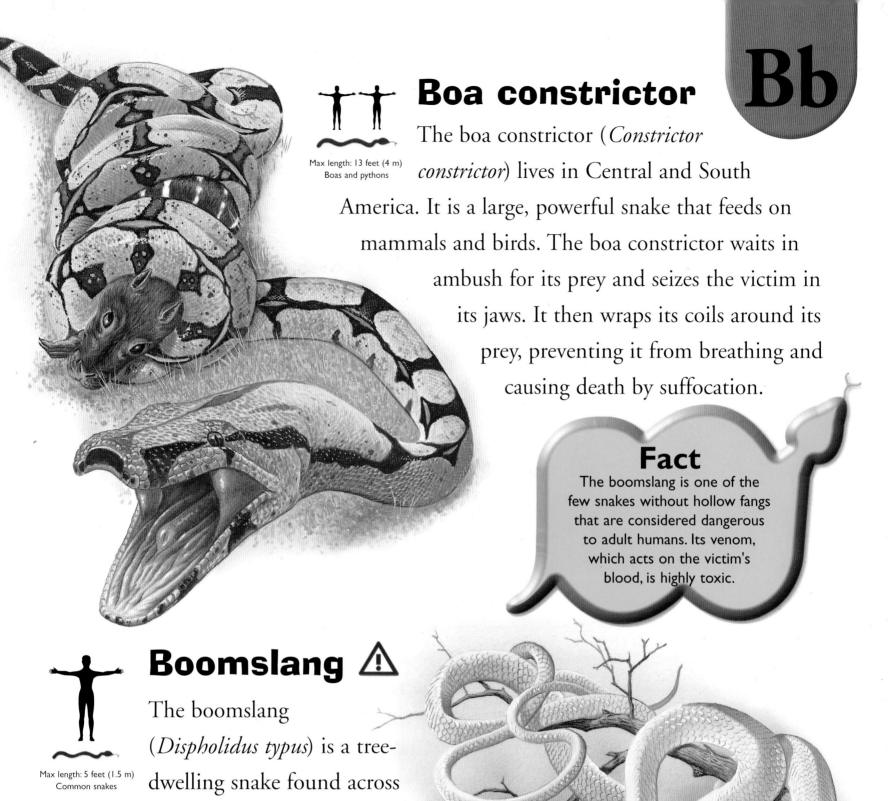

Boa constrictor

Max length: 13 feet (4 m)
Boas and pythons

The boa constrictor (*Constrictor constrictor*) lives in Central and South America. It is a large, powerful snake that feeds on mammals and birds. The boa constrictor waits in ambush for its prey and seizes the victim in its jaws. It then wraps its coils around its prey, preventing it from breathing and causing death by suffocation.

Fact
The boomslang is one of the few snakes without hollow fangs that are considered dangerous to adult humans. Its venom, which acts on the victim's blood, is highly toxic.

Boomslang ⚠

Max length: 5 feet (1.5 m)
Common snakes

The boomslang (*Dispholidus typus*) is a tree-dwelling snake found across most of Africa south of the Sahara Desert. It is very venomous, but its fangs are in the back of its mouth. The boomslang hunts lizards and birds in the trees. Its venom drips in as the snake chews its prey.

Brown tree snake ⚠

Max length: 7 feet 6 inches (2.3 m)
Vipers

The brown tree snake (*Boiga irregularis*), which is also known as the brown catsnake, is found in northern Australia, New Guinea, and parts of Indonesia. It spends most of its time in the trees hunting birds and small mammals. The brown tree snake has a venomous bite, but its venom is not strong enough to kill an adult human. However it is considered dangerous to children.

Max length: 10 feet (3 m)
Pit vipers

Bushmaster ⚠

The bushmaster (*Lachesis mutus*) is found in the forests of northern South America, and is the longest member of the viper family. Its venom is weak, but it produces an extremely large quantity, making this a dangerous snake. Fortunately, the bushmaster is generally shy and secretive, and hunts small mammals at night.

Calabar ground python

Max length: 3 feet (90 cm)
Boas and pythons

The Calabar ground python (*Calabaria reinhardtii*) spends most of its time below ground, hunting small mammals in its tunnels. When it ventures out, it has an unusual means of defense. The snake confuses predators by raising its tail, which is shaped almost exactly like its head.

Carpet python

Max length: 13 feet (4 m)
Boas and pythons

The carpet python (*Morelia spilotus*) lives in Australia and New Guinea. There are several variations, each with its own distinctive markings. It is active both during the day and at night, hunting, lizards, small mammals, and birds. Although it is not venomous, its powerful jaws can deliver a very painful bite.

Cascabel ⚠

Max length: 6 feet (1.8 m)
Pit vipers

The cascabel (*Crotalus durissus*), also known as the tropical rattlesnake, is found in Central and South America. It is active only at night, when it hunts small mammals using the heat-sensitive pits beneath its eyes. The cascabel is extremely poisonous and is responsible for dozens of human deaths each year.

 **Cc**

Cat-eyed snake

Max length: 2 feet 8 inches (81 cm)
Common snakes

The cat-eyed snake (*Leptodeira septentrionalis*) is found from the southernmost United States to northern South America. It gets its name from the distinctive vertical pupils in its eyes. The cat-eyed snake eats small animals and frog's eggs, and paralyzes its victims with a venomous bite. The venom is not very strong, and this snake is considered harmless to humans.

Chicken snake

Max length: 8 feet (2.4 m)
Common snakes

The chicken snake (*Spilotes pullatus*) is a large, tree-dwelling snake found in Central and South America. It is sometimes called the tiger ratsnake because of its variable black-and-yellow coloring which can look like bands on some individuals. The chicken snake is nonvenomous. It hunts birds and small reptiles, which it kills by constriction.

Copperhead

Max length: 4 feet (1.3 m)
Pit vipers

The copperhead (*Agkistrodon contortrix*) is a venomous snake found in the central and southeastern United States. It hunts mainly by night and feeds on frogs, lizards, and small mammals, which it kills with its venomous bite. The copperhead is dangerous, but its venom is not usually strong enough to kill a healthy adult human.

Corn snake

Max length: 6 feet (1.8 m)
Common snakes

The corn snake (*Elaphe guttata*) lives in the central and southeastern United States of America. It is usually found on the ground, beneath logs, or in leaf litter, but it is an excellent climber and may be found in trees or buildings. The corn snake feeds mainly on rats and mice that it hunts at night. Although it is considered harmless, it will bite if provoked.

Cottonmouth

Max length: 4 feet (1.2 m)
Pit vipers

The cottonmouth (*Agkistrodon piscivorus*) also known as the water moccasin, lives in and near water in the southeastern United States. The cottonmouth is very poisonous. Its venom is much stronger that that of its relative, the copperhead. It is not usually aggressive, but it will stand its ground with its mouth open, showing the white lining.

19

Dd

Max length: 5 feet (1.5 m)
Vipers

Daboia ⚠

The daboia (*Vipera russelli*), which is also known as Russell's viper, is found across India and Southeast Asia. It is extremely venomous, and is responsible for more human deaths each year than any other snake. It hunts small mammals at night, and hides in a tight coil during the day. If disturbed or provoked, the daboia strikes so hard that it lifts its whole body off the ground.

Dice snake

Max length: 3 feet 3 inches (1 m)
Common snakes

The dice snake (*Natrix tesselata*) is a close relative of the ringed snake, and is found from southern Europe to central Asia. It is an excellent swimmer and spends most of its time in water, where it hunts fish and amphibians. It is also known as the tessellated water snake because of its irregular coloration.

Fact
The dice snake is highly adapted to life in the water—both its eyes and its nostrils point upward, so it can keep most of its body submerged like a crocodile.

Egg-eating snake

Max length: 3 feet 3 inches (1 m)
Common snakes

The egg-eating snake (*Dasypeltis scabra*) lives in sub-Saharan Africa. It has very flexible jaws and no teeth. Instead it has hard projections at the back of its throat, which pierce the egg so the snake can crush the shell and swallow the contents. The shell is regurgitated after all the nutrition has been taken from the egg.

Egyptian cobra

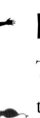

Max length: 8 feet (2.4 m)
Elapids

The Egyptian cobra (*Naja haje*), also known as the asp, is found around the edges of the Sahara Desert in northern, eastern, and western Africa. It is extremely poisonous, and its bite is deadly to humans. The Egyptian cobra hunts mainly at night, feeding on a wide variety of prey.

Fact
The ancient Egyptian queen Cleopatra is supposed to have committed suicide by letting herself be bitten by an Egyptian cobra.

Ee

Elephant's trunk snake

Max length: 8 feet (2.4 m)
Common snakes

The elephant's trunk snake (*Acrochordus javanicus*) lives in swamps, lakes, and streams in northern Australia, India, Southeast Asia, and New Guinea, where it hunts fish mainly at night. It is sometimes known as the file snake or wart snake, because of the tough, raised scales that cover its body. These specially adapted scales enable the elephant's trunk snake to wrap itself tightly around slippery fish.

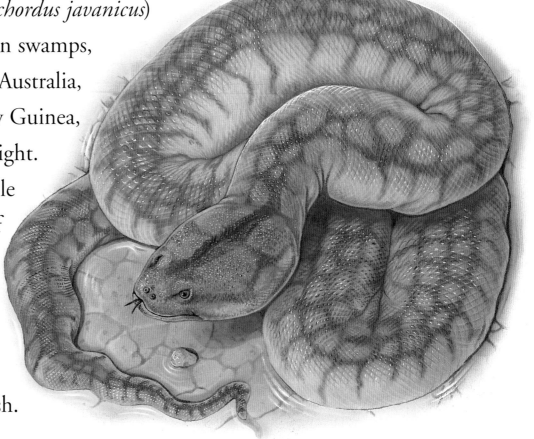

Emerald tree boa

Max length: 8 feet (2.4 m)
Boas and pythons

The emerald tree boa (*Corallus caninus*) lives in the tropical rainforests of northern South America. This nonvenomous snake is rarely seen on the ground. It coils itself around a tree branch and waits in ambush, perfectly camouflaged by its green-and-white coloration. When a bird or small mammal gets close enough, the snake extends its body and seizes its prey.

False water cobra ⚠️

Max length:
6 feet 6 inches (2 m)
Elapids

The false water cobra (*Hydrodynastes gigas*) is found in western South America. It is a venomous snake, but its fangs are in the back of its mouth, and its venom is weak. It takes its name from the fact that, like a true cobra, it spreads its neck when threatened.

Max length:
6 feet 6 inches (2 m)
Pit vipers

Fer-de-lance ⚠️

The fer-de-lance (*Bothrops atrox*) is a venomous snake from the forests of Central and South America. It is often found on agricultural land, where it hunts lizards and small mammals. The fer-de-lance is extremely aggressive, and its venom is considered highly dangerous to humans.

Flowerpot snake

Max length: 6 inches (15 cm)
Common snakes

The flowerpot snake (*Rhamphotyphlops braminus*) is a small burrowing snake, also known as the Brahminy blindsnake. It was originally found in southern Asia, but has spread to other parts of the world by being transported in the pots of houseplants. All flowerpot snakes are female and produce young without mating.

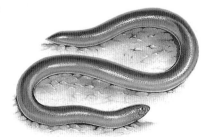

Flying snake

Max length: 4 feet (1.2 m)
Common snakes

The flying snake (*Chrysopela ornata*) lives in the forests of southern Asia. This small, nonvenomous, tree-dwelling snake cannot actually fly, but it can glide considerable distances. The snake spreads its body into a curved shape and launches itself into the air. Its body acts as a parachute, and the snake glides in a semicontrolled fall to a lower branch.

Fact

The flying snake can not only glide downward, it can leap more than 40 inches (one meter) between branches that are the same height above ground.

Max length: 4 feet 2 inches (1.3 m)
Common snakes

Fox snake

The fox snake (*Elaphe vulpine*) is found in the northern United States and parts of southern Canada. It is nonvenomous and is considered completely harmless because it rarely attempts to bite people, even when threatened. The fox snake feeds on small mammals, which it hunts on the ground and in burrows.

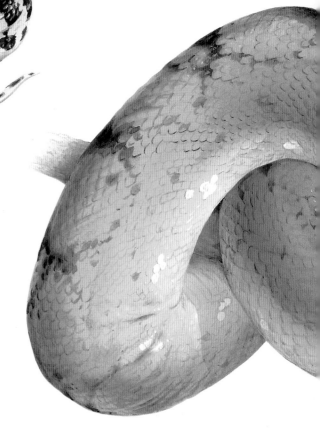

Gaboon viper ⚠

Max length: 6 feet 6 inches (2 m)
Pit vipers

The Gaboon viper (*Bitis gabonica*) is a ground-dwelling, venomous snake that lives in the equatorial rainforests of central Africa. Its complex markings make it very difficult to see among the leaves. It has the longest fangs in the snake world. The venom of the Gaboon viper is very powerful, and its lightning quick strike makes it dangerous to humans.

Garden tree boa

Max length: 6 feet 6 inches (2 m)
Boas and pythons

The garden tree boa (*Corallus hortulanus*) lives near riverbanks in the rainforests of South America, and is sometimes known as the Amazon tree boa. This nonvenomous snake has long teeth and wide jaws. It hunts mainly at night, sliding through the branches in search of prey such as birds, mammals, lizards, and frogs.

Garter snake

Max length: 4 feet (1.2 m)
Common snakes

The San Francisco garter snake (*Thamnophis sirtalis tetrataenia*) is the most colorful of the many different garter snakes that live in various parts of North America. It is also the most endangered, and is found only near San Francisco, California. Like other garter snakes, it is harmless and feeds on amphibians, fish, and other snakes.

Green snake

Max length: 3 feet (90 cm)
Common snakes

The rough green snake (*Opheodrys aestivus*) is found in the southeastern United States, living in woodlands near water. This snake is perfectly camouflaged for living in bushes and grassy areas, and is a good swimmer also. The rough green snake is nonvenomous and feeds mainly on insects such as grasshoppers and crickets.

Hairy bush viper ⚠

Max length: 2 feet (60 cm)
Vipers

The hairy bush viper (*Atheris hispida*) is a rare poisonous snake found in scattered populations in central Africa. It gets its name from the scales on its head and neck, which are raised into small points. This snake hunts mainly at night. It is extremely dangerous because there is no known antidote for its deadly venom.

Hognose snake

Max length: 2 feet (60 cm)
Common snakes

The eastern hognose snake (*Heterodon platirhinos*) has a thick body and an upturned snout. It is found across the eastern United States. If threatened, it first spreads its neck to form a hood, and hisses loudly. If this fails, it pretends to be dead.

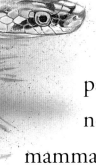

House snake

Max length: 3 feet (90 cm)
Common snakes

Fisk's house snake (*Lamprophis fiski*) is the rarest of the African house snakes, and is found only in a few parts of southeastern Africa. House snakes are nonvenomous, and feed on lizards and small mammals, especially rats and mice.

Ii

Indian cobra ⚠

Max length: 7 feet (2.1 m)
Elapids

The Indian cobra (*Naja naja*) is a highly venomous snake. Like other cobras, it raises its head and spreads its neck into a "hood" when it is threatened, then strikes quickly. The venom of the Indian cobra can be deadly, and kills many people each year. It feeds on rodents, lizards, and frogs.

Fact
Most Indian cobras have pale "eye" markings on the back of their hoods—these give the snake its other name, the spectacled cobra.

Indigo snake

Max length: 9 feet (2.7m)
Common snakes

The eastern indigo snake (*Drymarchon corais*) is found in parts of the southern United States. The indigo snake varies from its deep blue color to orange and red. It is nonvenomous and feeds on birds, small mammals, and other snakes. They are immune to the venom of all North American poisonous snakes.

Jade snake

Max length: 5 feet (1.5 m)
Common snakes

The jade snake (*Elaphe mandarina*), which is also known as the mandarin ratsnake, is found in southern China, Burma, and Vietnam. This nonvenomous snake has very distinctive yellow markings on its back. It prefers to live in mountain forests, where it hunts small mammals in their burrows. The jade snake is considered harmless to people.

Jararaca ⚠

Max length: 5 feet (1.5 m)
Pit vipers

The jararaca (*Bothrops jararaca*) is found along the eastern coast of central South America, in dry forests and grassland. It is a close relative of the fer-de-lance and is just as dangerous. The jararaca hunts frogs and small mammals on the ground. It is often found on farmland and is considered highly dangerous to humans.

Kk

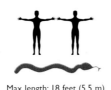

Max length: 18 feet (5.5 m)
Elapids

King cobra ⚠

The king cobra (*Ophiophagas hannah*), which is also known as the hamadryad, is the longest venomous snake in the world. It is found across southern and southeastern Asia, where it lives in thick forests, feeding mainly on other snakes. The king cobra is considered extremely dangerous and can deliver a large dose of venom, but it generally avoids human settlements.

Fact
A full-grown king cobra can lift its head high enough off the ground to look straight into the eyes of a man or woman who is standing upright.

Max length: 7 feet (2.1 m)
Common snakes

King snake

The common king snake (*Lampropeltis getula*) is found across the United States and in northern Mexico. It is nonvenomous and feeds mainly on small mammals and other snakes, including rattlesnakes. Like boas and pythons, king snakes kill their prey by constriction. There are several varieties of common king snake, and they may have plain, striped, or banded skins.

Krait ⚠

Max length:
7 feet 6 inches (3.3 m)
Elapids

The banded krait (*Bungarus fasciatus*) is a large venomous snake found across Southeast Asia. This snake has a raised backbone, so its body has an unusual triangular shape. The banded krait is shy and docile during the day, and will hide if it is disturbed. At night, however, it becomes aggressive and dangerous.

Leaf-nosed snake

Max length: 3 feet (90 cm)
Common snakes

The Madagascan leaf-nosed snake (*Langaha madagascariensis*) is the strangest-looking snake in the world. It is a tree dwelling snake with a narrow body and a very peculiar snout. The male has an elongated snout that comes to a sharp point, while the female has what looks like a small pinecone on its snout. These odd shapes help camouflage the snake while it waits to ambush lizards.

Kk
Ll

31

Levantine viper ⚠

Max length: 3 feet (90 cm)
Vipers

The Levantine viper (*Macrovipera lebetina*), also known as the blunt-nosed viper, is a highly venomous snake found in North Africa and the Middle East, and on a few Greek islands. It feeds on lizards, small mammals, and birds, which it hunts mainly on the ground, although it sometimes climbs into bushes. It is considered dangerous to humans.

Long-nosed tree snake ⚠

Max length: 4 feet (1.2 m)
Common snakes

The long-nosed tree snake (*Ahaetulla nasuta*) is a very slender snake that lives in the rain forests of Southeast Asia. Its long snout and horizontal pupils are very distinctive. The snake's green coloration gives it excellent camouflage as it hunts lizards among the branches. The long-nosed tree snake is venomous, but its venom is not strong enough to harm people.

Fact

When threatened, the long-nosed tree snake inflates its body so that its scales expand, revealing startling white markings underneath.

Max length: 3 feet (90 cm)
Pit vipers

Malayan pit viper ⚠

The Malayan pit viper (*Calloselasma rhodostoma*) is found in forest clearings and around the edges of farmland throughout Southeast Asia. This highly venomous snake hunts small mammals at night using the heat-sensitive organs in pits beneath its eyes. The venom of the Malayan pit viper is deadly to humans, and hundreds of people die each year after being bitten.

Max length: 6 feet 6 inches (2 m)
Common snakes

Malpolon ⚠

The malpolon (*Malpolon monspessulanus*), which is often known as the Montpelier snake, is found in southern Europe, along the coast of North Africa, and in southwestern Asia. It uses its large eyes to hunt its prey during the day. Although the malpolon is not considered dangerous, its bite is slightly venomous and usually requires medical attention.

Mm

Mamba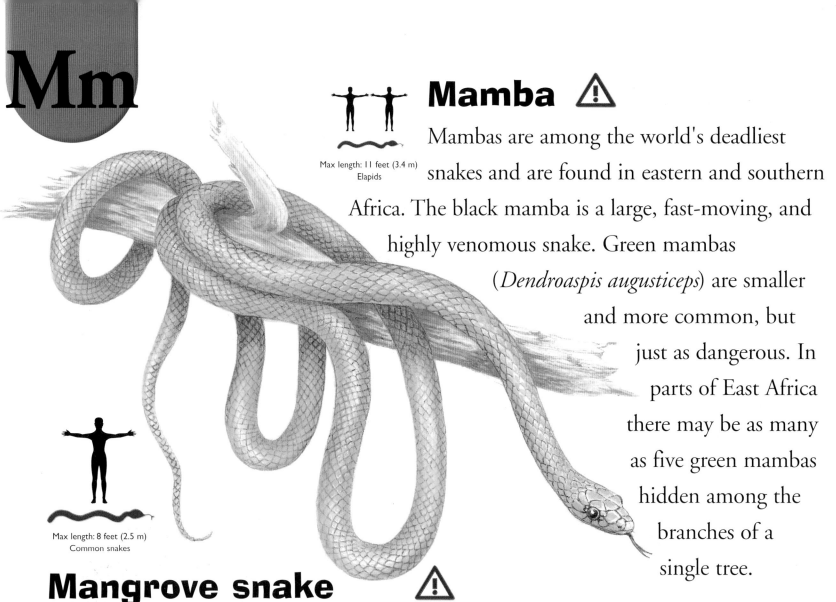

Max length: 11 feet (3.4 m)
Elapids

Mambas are among the world's deadliest snakes and are found in eastern and southern Africa. The black mamba is a large, fast-moving, and highly venomous snake. Green mambas (*Dendroaspis augusticeps*) are smaller and more common, but just as dangerous. In parts of East Africa there may be as many as five green mambas hidden among the branches of a single tree.

Max length: 8 feet (2.5 m)
Common snakes

Mangrove snake

The mangrove snake (*Boiga dendrophila*) is found in the hot, wet forests of Southeast Asia. It spends all its time in the trees, hunting birds, small mammals, and lizards; it also eats birds' eggs. The mangrove snake is venomous, but does not inject its venom through hollow fangs. Instead, the fangs are at the back of its mouth so it chews its prey to get venom into the wound.

Massasauga

Max length: 2 feet (60 cm)
Pit vipers

There are three species of massasauga, or pygmy rattlesnake (*Sistrurus species*), that are found in the central and southern United States and in northern Mexico. These small rattlesnakes prefer damp environments, such as swamps, where they hunt lizards, frogs, and small mammals. Despite their small size, massasaugas are considered dangerous because their venom is highly toxic.

Fact
Although massasaugas have rattles, the bony segments are so small that they make a buzzing sound rather than a rattle.

Mexican dwarf boa

Max length: 4 feet (1.2 m)
Boas and pythons

The Mexican dwarf boa (*Loxocemus bicolor*) is a rare nonvenomous snake that is also known as the Mexican burrowing snake. It feeds mainly on other snakes and small mammals, which it hunts underground by burrowing into their nests. This snake is also sometimes known as the neo-tropical sunbeam snake, because it looks like *Xenopeltis unicolor*, the sunbeam snake of Southeast Asia.

Max length: 6 feet (1.8 m)
Common snakes

Milk snake

The milk snake (*Lampropeltis triangulum nelfoni*) is found across most of the central, eastern, and southwestern United States, in Central America, and northern South America. There are more than 20 varieties, each with its own distinctive coloring. The milksnake is nonvenomous and feeds on small mammals and reptiles. Some of the varieties have colored bands that make them look like venomous coral snakes. They are often mistakenly killed for this reason.

Max length: 6 feet (1.8 m)
Common snakes

Mole snake

The mole snake (*Pseudapsis cana*) is a nonvenomous snake found in eastern and southern Africa. Its pointed snout and down-turned upper lip help it to burrow underground in search of small mammals such as moles and rats. Young mole snakes also eat lizards and certain species eat whole eggs. This snake is often mistaken for the cape cobra.

Mozambique spitting cobra ⚠

Max length: 5 feet (1.5 m)
Elapids

The Mozambique spitting cobra (*Naja Mossambica*) is the most common cobra in southern Africa, and the most deadly. It lives in a variety of locations including city parks. It shelters from the daytime sun beneath tree stumps and in old animal burrows. This snake hunts birds, lizards, and small mammals mainly at night. It defends itself by accurately spitting venom into their eyes.

Fact

A spitting cobra can spray its venom accurately up to 13 feet (4 m). The venom can cause permanent blindness if it is not immediately washed out with water.

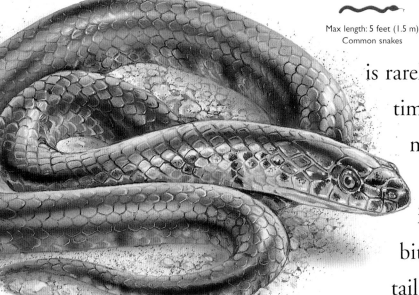

Mud snake

Max length: 5 feet (1.5 m)
Common snakes

The mud snake (*Farancia abacura*) lives in the southeastern United States. It is rarely seen, and spends most of its time around swamps and along muddy riverbanks, where it hunts for eels. The mud snake is nonvenomous and does not bite, but it has a sharp spine in its tail for defense against predators.

Max length: 8 feet (2.4 m)
Common snakes

Mussurana ⚠

The mussurana (*Clelia clelia clelia*) is a rare snake found in the rainforests of Central and South America. Adult snakes have a dark coloration, but young mussuranas are brightly colored and look like young coral snakes.

The mussurana feeds on lizards, snakes, and small mammals, which it kills with its venomous bite. Although venomous, the mussurana is not considered a danger to humans.

Max length: 2 feet (60 cm)
Pit vipers

Night adder ⚠

The night adder (*Causus rhombeatus*) is found throughout Africa south of the Sahara Desert. It is sometimes called the rhombic night adder because of the rhomboid (diamond-shaped) markings along its back. It hides in termite mounds during the day and emerges at night to hunt its prey.

Northern death adder

Max length: 3 feet (90 cm)
Elapids

The northern death adder (*Acanthophis praelongus*) lives in the eucalyptus forests and woodlands of northern Australia. It hunts birds, amphibians, and small mammals both by day and by night.

Though it resembles a viper, it belongs to the group that includes cobras and mambas. The venom of the northern death adder is more than strong enough to kill a person. This snake is very dangerous, and all bites should be treated as medical emergencies.

Nose-horned viper

Max length: 3 feet (90 cm)
Vipers

The nose-horned viper (*Vipera ammodytes*), which is also known as the long-nosed viper, is the most venomous snake in Europe. Its venom is strong enough to kill an adult human, and the distinctive upturned horn on its snout serves as a warning not to approach this dangerous snake. It is found around the northeastern coast of the Mediterranean Sea, and prefers to live high on rocky slopes, where it hunts lizards, birds, and small mammals.

Oo

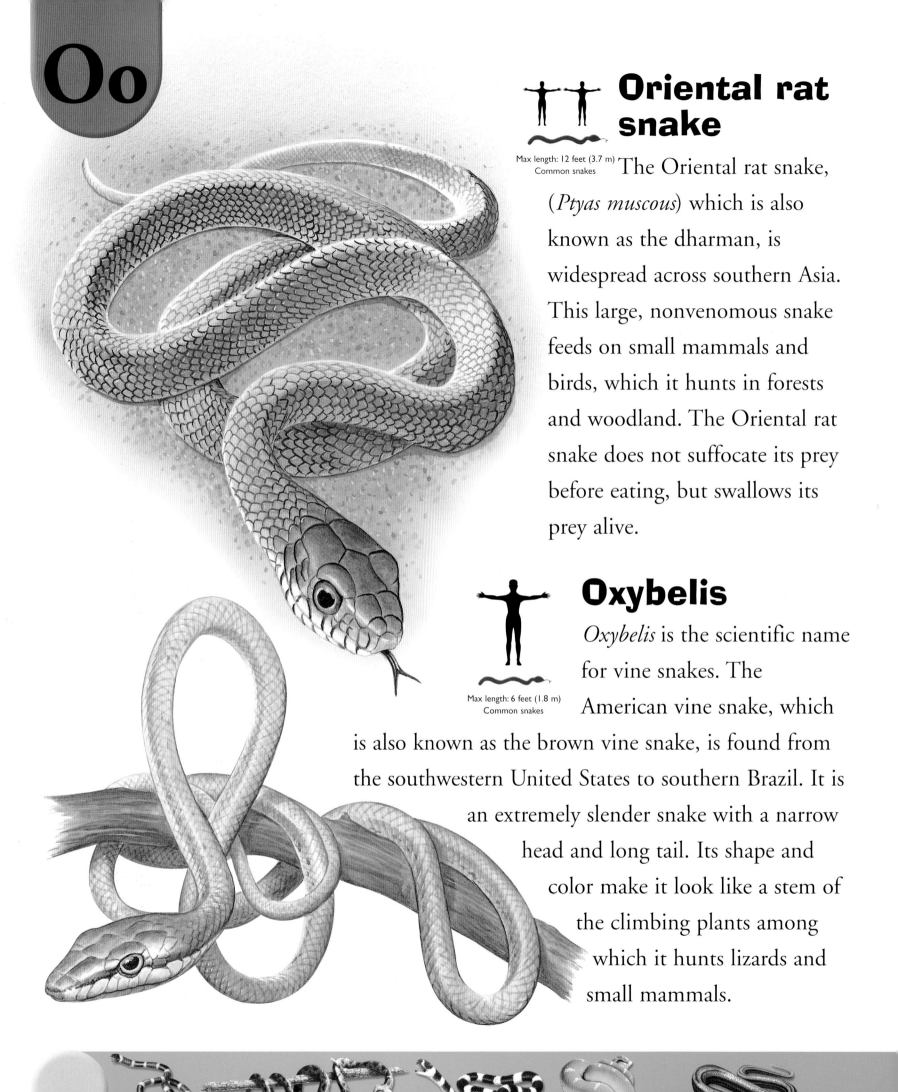

Oriental rat snake

Max length: 12 feet (3.7 m)
Common snakes

The Oriental rat snake, (*Ptyas muscous*) which is also known as the dharman, is widespread across southern Asia. This large, nonvenomous snake feeds on small mammals and birds, which it hunts in forests and woodland. The Oriental rat snake does not suffocate its prey before eating, but swallows its prey alive.

Oxybelis

Max length: 6 feet (1.8 m)
Common snakes

Oxybelis is the scientific name for vine snakes. The American vine snake, which is also known as the brown vine snake, is found from the southwestern United States to southern Brazil. It is an extremely slender snake with a narrow head and long tail. Its shape and color make it look like a stem of the climbing plants among which it hunts lizards and small mammals.

Patch-nosed snake

Max length: 3 feet (90 cm)
Common snakes

The Texas patch-nosed snake (*Salvadora grahamiae*) lives in the mountainous regions of the southwestern United States. It gets its name from the single upturned scale at the end of its snout. The mountain patch-nosed snake is nonvenomous and feeds on small lizards, which it hunts on the ground. This snake is not aggressive and prefers to hide if disturbed.

Fact
The patch-nosed snake is also known as the "striped racer" because of the speed it can reach when chasing lizards and insects across the rocky desert.

Pipe snake

Max length: 3 feet (90 cm)
Common snakes

The South American pipe snake (*Anilius scytale*) is a nonvenomous, burrowing snake found near water in the Amazonian rainforest. It feeds on other snakes, lizards, salamanders, frogs, and eels. The South American pipe snake is brightly colored to warn predators that it might be a highly venomous South American coral snake, but it is just a fake.

Pp

Max length: 3 feet (90 cm)
Pit vipers

Pope's tree viper ⚠

Pope's tree viper (*Trimeresurus popeorum*) is a venomous snake found in northern India and Southeast Asia, where it hunts lizards, amphibians, and small mammals. The green coloration of its scales help it to remain camouflaged in the trees. It is sometimes called Pope's pit viper—not because it lives in pits, but because of the heat-sensitive organs located in shallow depressions on the sides of its head.

Puff adder ⚠

Max length: 6 feet (1.8 m)
Pit vipers

The puff adder (*Bitis arietans*) is a heavy-bodied venomous snake found in central and southern Africa. Its name comes from the fact that when it is frightened, the snake puffs up its body with air, making it look even fatter than it is. The puff adder feeds mainly on birds and small mammals. Its venom is strong enough to kill a person, and this snake is considered extremely dangerous.

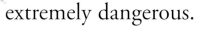

Qq

Queen snake

The queen snake (*Regina septemvittata*) is found in the eastern United States, from the Great Lakes to the Gulf of Mexico, but not in Florida. It lives near small ponds and streams, and spends most of its time in the water, hunting for crayfish. The queen snake is nonvenomous and is considered harmless.

Max length: 3 feet (90 cm)
Common snakes

Fact

Quill-nosed snakes were given their name because the shape of their heads is similar to an old-fashioned quill pen made from a sharpened feather.

Quill-nosed snake

Max length: 2 feet (60 cm)
Common snakes

Quill-nosed snakes (*Xenocalamus bicolor lineatus*) are found only in dry, sandy regions of southern Africa, especially the Kalahari Desert. These small, nonvenomous snakes have thin bodies, small eyes, and distinctive downturned, pointed snouts. Quill-nosed snakes spend most of their time burrowing through sand in search of the worm lizards on which they feed, and are rarely seen on the surface.

Max length: 5 feet (1.5 m)
Common snakes

Racer

The racer (*Coluber constrictor*) is found in North and Central America, with the exception of the western United States. It prefers open ground near lakes and fields. By snake standards, the racer is fast-moving (hence its name), but it is really quite slow. A racer's top speed is only about 4 mph (6.5 km/h)—about as fast as a person can walk.

Max length: 6 feet (1.8 m)
Boas and pythons

Rainbow boa

The rainbow boa (*Epicrates cenchria cenchria*) is found in South America, and there are several variations—the most colorful one lives in the Brazilian rainforest. The rainbow boa gets its name from the iridescent sheen of its scales. It is a nonvenomous snake that hunts small mammals at night, and kills its prey by constriction.

Rr

Red-bellied blacksnake ⚠

Max length: 9 feet (2.7 m)
Elapids

The red-bellied blacksnake (*Pseudechis porphyriacus*) is found in swamps and along riverbanks in eastern Australia. It feeds mainly on frogs, which it kills with its venomous bite, but it also hunts lizards and small mammals. The venom of the red-bellied blacksnake is strong enough to kill a person, and this snake is considered very dangerous.

Reticulated python

Max length: 33 feet (10 m)
Boas and pythons

The reticulated python (*Python reticulatus*) rivals the South American anaconda as the longest snake in the world. It is found throughout Southeast Asia, in forests and on grassland and farmland. The reticulated python is nonvenomous and feeds on wild pigs, monkeys, chickens, and small mammals, which it kills by suffocation in its powerful coils. Large reticulated pythons are dangerous, because people have been killed and eaten by these snakes, though it is rare.

Rhinoceros viper ⚠

Max length: 4 feet (1.2 m)
Vipers

The rhinoceros viper (*Bitis nasicornis*) is found in the tropical forests of western and central Africa. It gets its name from the two small "horns" on the end of its snout. This highly venomous snake is also known as the river jack, because it often waits to ambush small mammals at river crossings. It is a good swimmer and also hunts frogs along riverbanks.

Fact

The rhinoceros viper has complicated markings that make it very difficult to spot—this type of coloration is known as cryptic camouflage.

Ringed snake

Max length: 7 feet (2.1 m)
Common snakes

The ringed snake (*Natrix natrix*) is found throughout most of Europe and North Africa, and in parts of western Asia.

It is also known as the grass snake, but water snake would be a better description, because it is an excellent swimmer. It hunts frogs and small fish in streams and ponds. The ringed snake is not venomous, but will hiss and bite if threatened.

Ringneck snake

Max length: 3 feet (90 cm)
Common snakes

The ringneck snake (*Diadophis punctatus*) is found throughout the eastern and southern United States. This small, nonvenomous snake is rarely seen in the open. It prefers to hunt slugs and lizards beneath rocks and fallen trees. When threatened, the ringneck snake raises its head to display its bright underside and emits a foul-smelling substance.

Ringhal ⚠

Max length: 5 feet (1.5 m)
Elapids

The ringhal (*Hemachatus haemachatus*), which is sometimes spelled rinkhal, is a highly venomous snake found in southern Africa. It is one of the spitting cobras—as well as delivering a deadly bite, it can squirt its venom into the eyes of an enemy. Ringhals prefer to feed on frogs and toads, but will hunt small mammals and birds also.

Rosy boa

The rosy boa (*Charina trivirgata*) is a nonvenomous desert snake found in the southwestern United States and in northern Mexico. It hunts at night, seeking out small mammals and birds on the ground and in bushes and shrubs. The rosy boa has powerful jaws, but kills its prey by constriction. It is not aggressive and is considered harmless to humans.

Max length: 3 feet (90 cm)
Boas and pythons

Fact

Not all rosy boas are rosy—only a few individuals have stripes with the orange-red coloration that gives the snake its name.

Max length: 2 feet (60 cm)
Boas and pythons

Rubber boa

The rubber boa (*Charina bottae*) lives in the cooler regions of western North America, and is often found high on mountainsides. This nonvenomous snake spends most of its time on the ground, but can also burrow, swim, and climb trees to find food. The rubber boa feeds mainly on birds and small mammals, but it may also eat amphibians and small snakes.

Sand boa

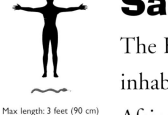

Max length: 3 feet (90 cm)
Boas and pythons

The Kenyan sand boa (*Eryx colubrinus*) inhabits dry grassland, and is found in northeastern Africa and the southern tip of the Arabian peninsula. This nonvenomous snake burrows through sand and loose soil in search of small mammals and nesting birds. Like other boas, the sand boa kills its prey by constriction.

Santa Catalina rattlesnake ⚠️

Max length: 2 feet (60 cm)
Pit vipers

The Santa Catalina rattlesnake (*Crotalus catalinensis*) is found only on the Mexican island of Santa Catalina in the Gulf of California. This snake is famous for being the "rattleless" rattlesnake. Instead of building up to form a rattle, as in the other rattlesnakes, the circular tail segments drop off after they have formed. The venom of the this snake is extremely strong and dangerous.

Ss

Saw-scaled viper ⚠

Max length: 3 feet (90 cm)
Vipers

The saw-scaled viper (*Echis carinatus*) is a highly venomous snake found in northern Africa, Iran, and the Indian subcontinent. It gets its name from its habit of rubbing its body against itself when threatened or alarmed. The snake's rough scales make a rasping sound like a saw cutting wood. The saw-scaled viper is extremely dangerous.

Sidewinder ⚠

Max length: 2 feet (60 cm)
Pit vipers

The sidewinder (*Crotalus cerastes*) is a venomous rattlesnake that lives in the deserts of the southwestern United States and northern Mexico. Along with a few other snakes, the sidewinder has a special way of moving—it moves sideways through a series of S-shaped loops. Using this method, the sidewinder can move quickly over sand. This method of locomotion also keeps most of the snake's body out of contact with the hot sand.

Slug-eating snake

Max length: 2 feet (60 cm)
Common snakes

The white-spotted slug-eating snake (*Pareas margaritophorus*) of southern China is one of about 40 snakes that specialize in eating slugs and snails. Slug-eating snakes are found in the rainforests of South America and Southeast Asia, and they are usually inactive during the day. At night, they hunt for prey on the ground and along tree branches.

Fact

The skull of a slug eating snake is different to other snakes. It has a rigid lower jaw that allows it to scoop snails out of their shells.

Smooth snake

Max length: 2 feet (60 cm)
Common snakes

The smooth snake (*Coronella austriaca*) is widespread throughout western Asia and most of Europe, except for Britain where it is extremely rare. It feeds mainly on lizards, which it hunts during the day in dry, rocky places, but it will also eat small mammals. The smooth snake is nonvenomous and kills its prey by constriction.

Ss

South American coral snake ⚠

Max length: 5 feet (1.5 m)
Elapids

The South American coral snake (*Micrurus lemniscatus*) is found throughout the forests and grasslands of northern South America. It usually lives near water and feeds on fish, frogs, and lizards. This snake is highly venomous and is considered extremely dangerous. Its bright coloration warns predators—and people—to stay away.

Fact
The stinking goddess is the world's smelliest snake—its foul odor is detectable for hundreds of yards (meters).

Stinking goddess

Max length: 6 feet (1.8 m)
Common snakes

The stinking goddess (*Elaphe carinata*) is an aggressive and very smelly snake that is found only in China and Taiwan. It lives in hilly bamboo forests and feeds mainly on other snakes. Although it is nonvenomous and not considered dangerous, it is a very unpleasant snake. If disturbed, it hisses, puffs up its body, emits a foul-smelling substance, and bites repeatedly.

Taipan ⚠

Max length: 13 feet (4 m)
Elapids

The taipan (*Oxyuranus scutellatus*) is one of the world's deadliest snakes—the venom injected by a single bite is strong enough to kill a dozen people. The taipan is found in open woodlands and sugarcane fields of northern Australia and southern New Guinea, where it hunts small mammals on the ground. This extremely dangerous snake is quite rare.

Tentacled snake ⚠

Max length: 3 feet (90 cm)
Common snakes

The tentacled snake (*Erpeton tentaculatum*) is a very unusual-looking snake that lives in the rivers of Southeast Asia. It is thought that the two fleshy "tentacles" on its snout are used for locating fish and frogs under water. The snake can remain submerged for more than five minutes before returning to the surface to breathe. The tentacled snake kills its prey with venom, but it is not dangerous to humans.

Tt

Timber rattlesnake ⚠

Max length: 6 feet (1.8 m)
Pit vipers

The timber rattlesnake (*Crotalus horridus*) lives in the eastern United States, except Florida. It is usually found in mountain forests, but it also inhabits swamps and marshy ground. When disturbed, it rattles the loose segments at the end of its tail as a warning. The timber rattlesnake is venomous. Its habitat is being destroyed and its numbers are dropping.

Tree racer

Max length: 8 feet (2.4 m)
Common snakes

The red-tailed racer (*Gonysoma oxycephala*) is a nonvenomous, tree-dwelling snake that lives in the rainforests of Southeast Asia. It can move quickly enough to catch bats in mid-air and also hunts birds and small mammals, which it kills by constriction. When alarmed by a predator, the red-tailed racer inflates an air sac in its neck and opens its jaws wide, threatening to strike.

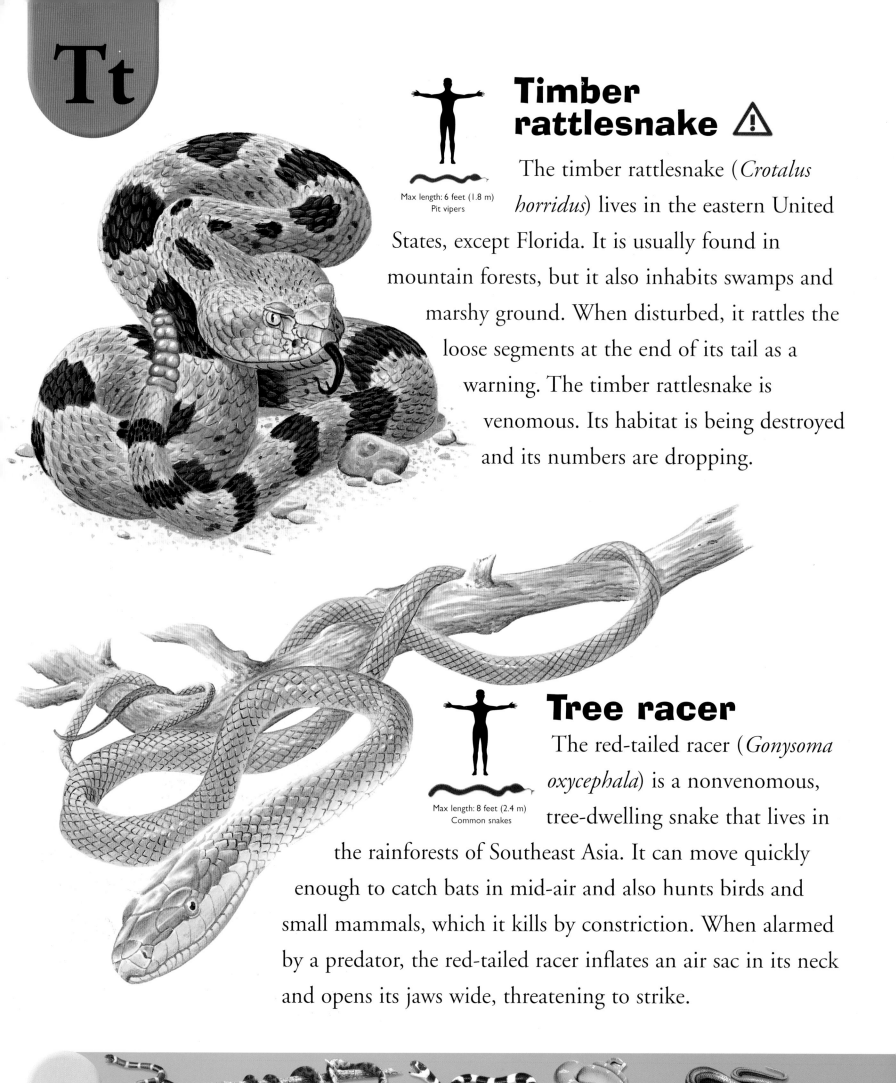

Twig snake ⚠️

Max length: 3 feet (90 cm)
Common snakes

The twig snake (*Thelotornis species*) lives in the rain forests of central and western Africa, where it hunts small mammals and birds in the trees. The twig snake is highly venomous. It chews its victim to get the venom into the wound. It can also inflate its throat area as a defensive display.

Fact

There is no antidote to twig snake venom—human victims usually die within about five days of being bitten.

Max length: 3 feet (90 cm)
Boas and pythons

Ungaliophis

Ungaliophis is the scientific name for the dwarf boas of Central America. These small, nonvenomous snakes feed on lizards, birds, and small mammals, which they hunt in rainforest trees. These snakes are known as banana boas, because they are sometimes unintentionally transported to Europe and North America in shipments of bananas.

Max length: 2 feet (60 cm)
Common snakes

Uropeltis

Uropeltis is the scientific name for the shield-tailed snakes, which are found only in southern India and Sri Lanka. These nonvenomous, burrowing snakes feed mainly on earthworms that they find underground. The snakes get their name from the tough, bony "shield" located at the end of their stumpy tails.

Max length: 6 feet (1.8 m)
Pit vipers

Urutu

The urutu, (*Bothrops alternatus*), which is also known as the cruchera, is a close relative of the fer-de-lance and the jararaca. It is found in the uplands of eastern South America, where it feeds on small mammals and birds. The highly dangerous urutu has hollow front fangs for injecting its deadly venom.

Viperine snake

The viperine snake (*Natrix maura*) is found in rivers and lakes in southwestern Europe and northwestern Africa. This nonvenomous, fish-eating snake was given its name because it looks and behaves like the venomous adder (common viper). When threatened, the viperine snake strikes like an adder, but keeps its mouth closed and does not bite.

Max length: 3 feet (90 cm)
Common snakes

Max length: 4 feet (1.2 m)
Vipers

Wagler's viper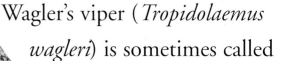

Wagler's viper (*Tropidolaemus wagleri*) is sometimes called the temple viper, because it is the snake that lives in the famous snake temple on the island of Penang in Malaysia. It is a venomous, tree-dwelling snake that prefers to live in swampy woodland in parts of Southeast Asia, Indonesia, and the Philippines. The venom of Wagler's viper is powerful and more than strong enough to kill a person.

Ww

Water snake

Max length: 5 feet (1.5 m)
Common snakes

There are several variations of water snake—some live in freshwater streams and ponds, while others prefer coastal salt marshes and lagoons. The southern water snake (*Nerodia fasciata*) is found in the southeastern United States. It feeds on fish and amphibians and is nonvenomous, but bites and releases foul-smelling fluid if attacked.

Western diamondback rattlesnake ⚠

Max length: 7 feet (2.1 m)
Pit vipers

The western diamondback rattlesnake (*Crotalus atrox*) is found in the southwestern United States and in northern Mexico. It feeds on lizards, small mammals, and birds. The western diamondback rattlesnake is one of the most dangerous snakes in North America. It injects large amounts of very strong venom, and several people die each year from this snake's bite.

Whipsnake

Max length: 8 feet (2.4 m)
Common snakes

The Alameda whipsnake (*Masticophis lateralis euryxanthus*) is one of the many varieties of whipsnake that live in the southern and western United States. The snakes get their group name from the pattern of scales on their long tails, which makes them look like braided leather whips. The Alameda whipsnake, or striped racer, is found only near San Francisco, California.

Like the other whipsnakes, it is nonvenomous and feeds on lizards, birds, and small mammals.

Wolf snake

Max length: 3 feet (90 cm)
Common snakes

The common wolf snake (*Lycodon capucinus*) lives in Southeast Asia, where it is often found near houses and in gardens. Other species of wolf snake live throughout Africa. All wolf snakes are nonvenomous and feed mainly on lizards. They get their name from the enlarged front teeth with which they seize their prey.

Xx

Max length: 4 feet (1.2 m)
Common snakes

Xenodon rhabdocephalus

This nonvenomous snake is better known as the false fer-de-lance, and is found in Central and South America. It closely resembles the highly dangerous fer-de-lance that lives in the same part of the world. The false fer-de-lance eats toads, and its back teeth are hinged to get a good grip on toads that puff themselves up when they are caught.

Xenopeltis unicolor

Max length: 4 feet (1.2 m)
Common snakes

Xenopeltis unicolor is a nonvenomous burrowing snake that is found throughout Southeast Asia. It spends most of its time underground, hunting for lizards and small mammals, and only comes to the surface after heavy rain. Its popular name is the sunbeam snake, because in sunlight its scales gleam with iridescent colors.

Yellow-bellied sea snake

Max length: 5 feet (1.5 m)
Elapids

The yellow-bellied sea snake (*Pelamis platurus*) is found in both the Indian and Pacific oceans. It is also known as the pelagic sea snake, because it is the only sea snake found in the open ocean—sometimes thousands of individuals gather at the surface. The yellow and black coloring warns sharks that this snake is venomous, so they leave it alone.

Fact
When the Californian mountain kingsnake moves, the colored bands blur into each other and appear greenish—this is known as interference camouflage.

Zonata

Max length: 3 feet (90 cm)
Common snakes

Lampropeltis zonata is the scientific name for the Californian mountain king snake, which is found in the coastal mountain forests of the southwestern United States. This nonvenomous snake feeds on birds, lizards, and other snakes. It is sometimes called the coral king snake because its vivid colors warn predators that it might be a poisonous coral snake.

Glossary

Amphibian An air-breathing animal with a backbone, which lays its eggs in water or moist places. Frogs, toads, newts, and salamanders are the most commonly encountered types of amphibian.

Antidote A drug that is intended to counteract the effects of a particular poison and cure the victim. Antidotes to snake venom are also called anti-venoms.

Camouflage Shape, color, and pattern that help an animal blend in with its background, so that its enemies—and its prey—cannot see it easily.

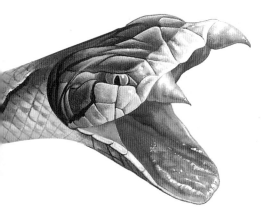

Cold-blooded animals Those that rely on their environment to maintain their body temperature. Fish, amphibians, and reptiles are the major groups of cold-blooded animals.

Constriction The method by which some snakes kill their prey. The snake coils tightly around its victim to prevent it from inflating its lungs and breathing. Death is caused by suffocation.

Equatorial Belonging to the hottest region of the Earth, near the equator.

Fang A long, sharp tooth designed for seizing prey. Many snakes have hollow fangs that inject venom when they bite.

Hibernate In cool climates, many animals spend the winter months in a type of long-term sleep known as hibernation. While they hibernate, their body functions slow down and they survive without food.

Invertebrates Animals that do not have an internal skeleton with a backbone. Insects, spiders, worms, and snails are invertebrates.

Iridescent Producing bright rainbow colors when viewed in sunlight. The colors often change if the angle of light or viewpoint changes.

Jaws The bones and muscles that surround the mouth of an animal. Most animals have jaws lined with teeth that are adapted to the sort of food they eat. Snakes do not chew their food, but some have backward curved teeth to hold onto their prey. Some snakes can expand their jaws to swallow food that is wider than the snake's own body.

Glossary

Juvenile An animal that is not full-grown.

Lizard A small to medium-sized reptile. Most lizards have four legs and a tail, but some lizards are legless and look like very short snakes.

Mammal A warm-blooded animal that produces live-born young. Only small mammals are hunted by snakes, but all mammals are vulnerable to venom from snake bites.

Molecule The smallest naturally occurring particle of any substance. Most molecules are made of a number of different atoms joined together. Animals with an extremely good sense of taste or smell can detect single molecules drifting in air or water.

Organ Part of an animal's body that does a special job. A snake uses lungs for breathing, eyes for seeing, and Jacobson's organ for sampling the air.

Predator An animal that hunts other animals.

Prey An animal that is hunted and eaten by others.

Pupil The dark central part of an eye through which light enters.

Reptile An air-breathing, cold-blooded animal with a backbone and scaly skin such as a snake, lizard, crocodile, or turtle.

Ribs The part of an animal's skeleton that protects the major internal organs (such as the heart and the lungs). A snake's ribs protrude from each side of the spine and are flexible so it can swallow large prey.

Rodent One of a group of small mammals that includes, mice, rats, and squirrels, but not shrews or rabbits.

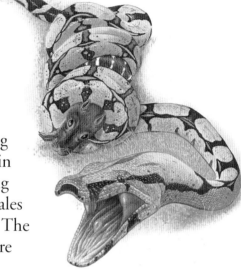

Scales Small, overlapping plates that protect the skin of some animals including fish and snakes. Snake scales can be smooth or rough. The scales on a snake's head are called scutes.

Suffocation To cause death by preventing a victim from breathing.

Tropical Belonging to the geographical region around the equator, between the Tropic of Cancer and the Tropic of Capricorn.

Venom A poison produced by an animal to kill its prey or as a defense mechanism.

Warm-blooded animals Those that use some of the energy they get from food to maintain their body temperature at a constant level. Mammals and birds are warm-blooded.

Index

A

Adder 10
Aesculapian snake 10
Anaconda 11
Antiguan racer 11
Arizona coral snake 12
Australian tiger snakc 12

B

Ball python 13
Bandy-bandy 13
Blindsnake 13
Blood python 14
Blue Malaysian coral snake 14
Boa constrictor 15
Boomslang 15
Brown tree snake 16
Bushmaster 16

C

Calabar ground python 17
Carpet python 17
Cascabel 17
Cat-eyed snake 18
Chicken snake 18
Copperhead 19
Corn snake 19
Cottonmouth 19

D E

Daboia 20
Dice snake 20
Egg-eating snake 21
Egyptian cobra 21
Elephant's trunk snake 22
Emerald tree boa 22

F

False water cobra 23
Fer-de-lance 23
Flowerpot snake 23
Flying snake 24
Fox snake 24

G

Gaboon viper 25
Garden tree boa 25
Garter snake 26
Green snake 26

H

Hairy bush viper 27
Hognose snake 27
House snake 27

I J

Indian cobra 28
Indigo snake 28
Jade snake 29
Jararaca 29

K L

King cobra 30
King snake 30
Krait 31
Leaf-nosed snake 31
Levantine viper 32
Long-nosed tree snake 32

M

Malayan pit viper 33
Malpolon 33
Mamba 34
Mangrove snake 34
Massasauga 35
Mexican dwarf boa 35
Milk snake 36
Mole snake 36
Mozambique spitting cobra 37
Mud snake 37
Mussurana 38

N

Night adder 38
Northern death adder 39
Nose-horned viper 39

O P

Oriental rat snake 40
Oxybelis 40
Patch-nosed snake 41
Pipe snake 41
Pope's tree viper 42
Puff adder 42

Q R

Queen snake 43
Quill-nosed snake 43
Racer 44
Rainbow boa 44
Red-bellied blacksnake 45
Reticulated python 45
Rhinoceros viper 46
Ringed snake 46
Ringneck snake 47
Ringhal 47
Rosy boa 48
Rubber boa 48

S

Sand boa 49
Santa Catalina rattlesnake 49
Saw-scaled viper 50
Sidewinder 50
Slug-eating snake 51
Smooth snake 51
South American coral snake 52
Stinking goddess 52

T

Taipan 53
Tentacled snake 53
Timber rattlesnake 54
Tree racer 54
Twig snake 55

U V

Ungaliophis 55
Uropeltis 56
Urutu 56
Viperine snake 57

W

Wagler's viper 57
Water snake 58
Western diamondback rattlesnake 58
Whipsnake 59
Wolf snake 59

X Y Z

Xenodon rhabdocephalus 60
Xenopeltis unicolor 60
Yellow-bellied sea snake 61
Zonata 61